A Reflective
f...
Children and Teens

Diana Hamlett, B.A. Sociology
Sonja Sharif, M. Ed. Reading Specialist

This journal is dedicated to:

Grief is a natural response to a loss.

Grief can make you feel sadness, pain, anger, fear, or loneliness.

Grief may be felt because someone you loved has died, is incarcerated, moved away, or is suffering from an illness.

Grief can also occur after experiencing a disaster or instances of abuse.

Someone/something special to me is gone.

I lost my:

_____

I felt_____

_____when I heard that

_____was gone.

Here are some of the thoughts and dreams I have had since I lost you…

Here are some memories of the times we spent together. I remember when we…

Some of the places we used to go were:

Some of the things you have taught me to do:

I really want to tell you:

I plan to do many great things. Some of my goals are:

Things that make me angry:

Things that make me sad:

Things that make me smile and calm me down:

Some of the feelings I have had are:

When I feel angry, I can:

When I feel afraid, the people I will go to are:

Some things I can do to help myself feel better:

Some of the things I still enjoy doing are:

Today was a difficult day for me because:

Write a letter to the person/thing that is gone:

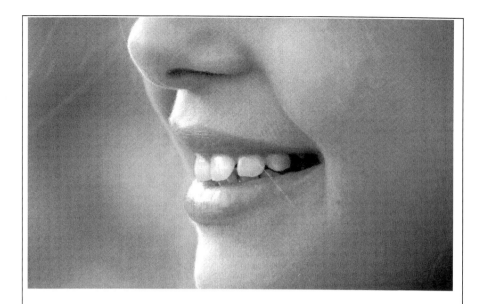

Here is an exercise you can try when you feel overwhelmed:

Just breathe…

1. Breathe through your nose.
2. Take a deep breath.
3. Hold your breath for 2 seconds.
4. Slowly breathe out though your mouth
5. Repeat until you feel better.
6. Smile.

Sometimes exercising makes us feel better.

Things you can do:

1. Stretch
2. Run
3. Walk
4. Jog
5. Play
6. Dance
7. Have fun; Get silly

Relax…

1.Stay calm.

2.Get a good night's sleep.

3.Read a book.

4.Draw a picture.

5.Listen to music.

Stay positive…

1. Believe things will get better in time.
2. Try new things.
3. Find a new hobby.
4. Journal.
5. Write poetry.
6. Think good thoughts.

Mood Tracker: Draw a face or write a word to express how you feel in the box.

Sun	Mon	Tue	Wed	Thu	Fri	Sat

Here are some words to describe how you may feel. Use these or choose your own.

sad upset angry mad annoyed

heartbroken happy troubled

peaceful calm sorry depressed

Mood Tracker: Draw a face or write a word to express how you feel in the box.

Sun	Mon	Tue	Wed	Thu	Fri	Sat

Here are some words to describe how you may feel. Use these or choose your own.

sad upset angry mad annoyed

heartbroken happy troubled

peaceful calm sorry depressed

Mood Tracker: Draw a face or write a word to express how you feel in the box.

Sun	Mon	Tue	Wed	Thu	Fri	Sat

Here are some words to describe how you may feel. Use these or choose your own.

sad upset angry mad annoyed

heartbroken happy troubled

peaceful calm sorry depressed

Mood Tracker: Draw a face or write a word to express how you feel in the box.

Sun	Mon	Tue	Wed	Thu	Fri	Sat

Here are some words to describe how you may feel. Use these or choose your own.

sad upset angry mad annoyed

heartbroken happy troubled

peaceful calm sorry depressed

Mood Tracker: Draw a face or write a word to express how you feel in the box.

Sun	Mon	Tue	Wed	Thu	Fri	Sat

Here are some words to describe how you may feel. Use these or choose your own.

sad upset angry mad annoyed

heartbroken happy troubled

peaceful calm sorry depressed

Mood Tracker: Draw a face or write a word to express how you feel in the box.

Sun	Mon	Tue	Wed	Thu	Fri	Sat

Here are some words to describe how you may feel. Use these or choose your own.

sad upset angry mad annoyed

heartbroken happy troubled

peaceful calm sorry depressed

Mood Tracker: Draw a face or write a word to express how you feel in the box.

Sun	Mon	Tue	Wed	Thu	Fri	Sat

Here are some words to describe how you may feel. Use these or choose your own.

sad upset angry mad annoyed

heartbroken happy troubled

peaceful calm sorry depressed

Mood Tracker: Draw a face or write a word to express how you feel in the box.

Sun	Mon	Tue	Wed	Thu	Fri	Sat

Here are some words to describe how you may feel. Use these or choose your own.

sad upset angry mad annoyed

heartbroken happy troubled

peaceful calm sorry depressed

Draw a picture

Made in the USA
Las Vegas, NV
01 February 2023

66648732R00024